CITY-STATES OF THE SWAHILI COAST

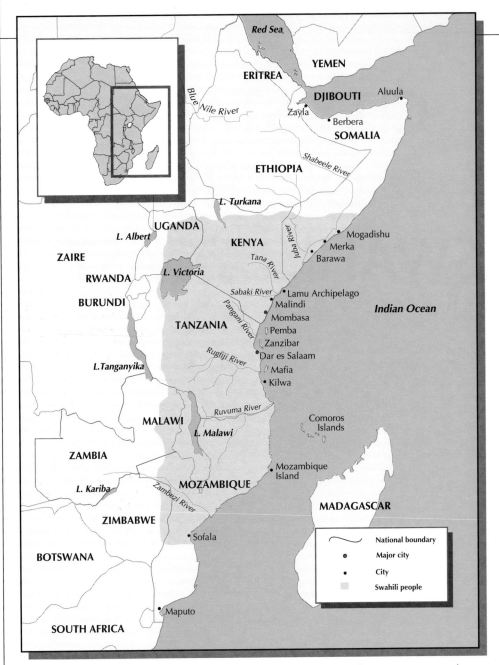

The Swahili Coast was inhabited by many city-states and towns sharing a common culture.

~African Civilizations~

CITY-STATES OF THE SWAHILI COAST

Thomas H. Wilson, Ph.D.

A First Book

Franklin Watts
A Division of Grolier Publishing
New York / London / Hong Kong / Sydney
Danbury, Connecticut

Library of Congress Cataloging-in-Publication Data

Wilson, Thomas H.
    City states of the Swahili coast / Thomas Wilson. — 1st ed.
        p.   cm. — (A first book)   (African civilizations)
    Includes bibliographical references and index.
    Summary: Discusses the history and culture of the Swahili peoples
    living along the eastern coast of Africa, from present-day Somalia to
    Mozambique.
    ISBN 0-531-20281-X
    1. Africa, Eastern—History—Juvenile literature. 2. Indian Coast
    (Africa)—History—Juvenile literature. [1. Africa, Eastern—History.]
    I. Title. II. Series III. Series: African civilizations.
    DT365.65.W55   1998
    967.6'00496392—dc21   97-37569
                                                     CIP
                                                     AC

CONTENTS

INTRODUCTION

The towns and cities of the Swahili Coast of East Africa stretch from present-day Somalia in the north to Mozambique in the south. This coast, which is about 2,000 miles (3,200 km) long, has ports for ships carrying trade goods across the Indian Ocean. For 1,200 years communities living along this coast grew rich from trade. They traded African products for items imported from Arab countries along the Red Sea and the Persian Gulf. They traded for goods from as far away as India, Southeast Asia, and China.

The civilization that grew up along this coast is called Swahili. It got its name from its people, most of whom spoke Swahili. A beautiful and poetic language, Swahili is one of a large group of *Bantu* languages that are spoken throughout central,

This section of the Swahili Coast is in the present-day country of Tanzania. The mangrove trees at the water's edge grow in muddy conditions along protected shorelines. Their roots reach above the ground to absorb air.

southern, and much of eastern Africa. Although Swahili is an African language, many of its words come from the Arabic language. This is a result of the centuries of trade that occurred between the coastal peoples of East Africa and the Arab world. The Swahili language can be written either in Arabic script or using the *Roman alphabet*.

The Swahili people are defined by the fact that they all speak the same language, follow the religion of *Islam*, and have a *multifaceted*, shared culture. In

The religious center of the Muslim world is Mecca in present-day Saudi Arabia. The Great Mosque, or Haram, in Mecca encloses the Kaaba, a draped cube that is the most important site of Muslim worship.

spite of their common culture, the Swahili towns never united into one empire or state. However, they often did cooperate with each other to achieve common goals.

The earliest Swahili settlements were founded in about A.D. 800. At that time the settlements were little more than small fishing villages or hamlets, with small economies and just the beginnings of long-distance trade. The trading settlements grew rapidly in number. It is estimated that by 1500 there were more than three hundred towns. Some towns were quite large, covering up to 70 acres (28 hectares) or more. The remains of these old Swahili towns dot the East African coast today, including   of palaces, grand houses, monumental tombs, and *mosques*. The largest of the towns became *city-states*.

In 1498 the Portuguese arrived on the Swahili Coast. They tried to take control of Swahili trading networks but succeeded only in damaging them. The Portuguese forced each Swahili town to choose either to support or defy them. This resulted in war between the towns. Soon other foreign powers entered the area. Their rivalries caused further disruptions among the Swahili. Although the Swahili continue to be traders to this day, their economy never recovered from these upheavals in the 1500s and 1600s.

Many Swahili communities still exist up and down the East African coast, including Lamu, Mombasa, and Zanzibar. Their common culture includes the Swahili language, Islam, a shared *worldview*, and twelve centuries of history.

ENVIRONMENT

The coastal environment of Swahili civilization had a great deal to do with its development. Swahili towns were usually on the coast and were rarely more than 2 miles (3.2 km) inland. They dotted the whole length of the 2,000-mile (3,219-km) coast, forming a long but narrow coastal corridor. Each town was also a gateway to the African interior. This allowed Swahili towns to control long-distance trade, both from overseas and from far inland.

MONSOON WINDS

Among the most important natural factors in the development of Swahili civilization were the winds.

The Swahili are famous for their ability as sailors.

Overseas trade was made possible by a pattern of seasonal winds in the Indian Ocean and Southeast Asia. These winds are known as monsoon winds or trade winds.

From approximately November to March, northeast monsoon winds filled the sails of ships coming to East Africa from the north and east. After about a month the trade winds reversed. From about May to September the southeast monsoon winds allowed trading vessels to sail northward. After another month or so without winds, the annual cycle began again.

The monsoon cycle allowed the Swahili to trade

with foreigners from ports along the coast of the Red Sea, South Arabia, the Persian Gulf, India, Southeast Asia, and China. The Swahili and the people from these ports both used the monsoon winds to sail back and forth. The winds also encouraged trading voyages up and down the East African coast between the Swahili towns themselves.

LOCAL ENVIRONMENTS

The East African coast is one long geographical feature, but local environments differ widely. Reliable winds for sailing, fresh water supplies, and good farmland encouraged the development of Swahili settlements.

The Swahili sought out natural harbors and reefs that protected anchored boats and provided good fishing grounds. They used coral from the reefs as building material—first by cutting blocks of coral and later by mixing crushed coral with lime and sand to create a concrete-like building material.

The Swahili also looked for natural resources that could be traded, such as ivory and skins.

Man on the island of Lamu loads blocks of cut coral to use for construction.

Mangroves, bush-like trees that grow in salt water along East African shores, provided timber useful for building. These were also valuable for export.

Arab geographers divided the coast into three areas, each with cultural, historical, and geographical differences. In the north was the Benadir coast (meaning the land of ports). Today this area is southern Somalia. The Land of Zanj (or the land of the blacks), was in the middle, and consisted of

The architecture of Mogadishu, Somalia, is closely related to that of Yemen (above), which is situated on the southern Arabian Peninsula. This similarity—one among many—is the result of centuries-old links between the Swahili Coast and Arab countries.

the coasts of modern-day Kenya and Tanzania. To the south was Sofala (the coast of shoals), the shore of present-day Mozambique.

THE BENADIR COAST

The most important ports on the Benadir coast were and still are Mogadishu, Merka, and Barawa in Somalia. They are situated on a long, bare coastline with mostly unprotected anchorages that are typical of the Benadir coast. The Shabeele River flows inland, providing fresh water for farming the fertile land.

Historical sources suggest that early inhabitants of this area may have been herders of camels or cattle. Today the *Cushitic*-speaking Somali and Oromo peoples herd camels and cattle in this region.

In southern Somalia many small islands create a protected sea-lane between the islands and the coast. This is ideal for small boats. Many Swahili villages sprang up on these islands.

THE LAND OF ZANJ

Even today, the Land of Zanj corresponds with that part of the coast where a cultural change occurs. The Cushitic-speakers of the north give way to the Bantu-speaking peoples who are spread throughout Africa south of the Sahara Desert.

The Zanj coast began in northern Kenya. There, the islands of the Lamu Archipelago offer protection for boats, good fishing grounds, plentiful building materials, and a wealth of plant and animal life. The island towns of Pate, Manda, and

A recent view of Zanzibar, in Tanzania

Shanga are some of the oldest and largest Swahili settlements along the entire coast.

Many towns developed on the central Kenyan coast near the mouths of creeks or rivers flowing into the Indian Ocean. Ungwana, Gedi, and Mtwapa are examples of these towns. The next great port to the south is Mombasa, which began as a Swahili community about 1,000 years ago. Today it is Kenya's second largest city and one of Africa's great ports.

The coast of Tanzania is dominated by the three large offshore islands of Pemba, Zanzibar, and

Mafia. Major Swahili cities and towns grew up on the mainland opposite them. Kilwa, another great Swahili city, developed in southern Tanzania on a small island close to the mainland.

Inland, Swahili communities usually had non-Swahili neighbors, who often lived in or visited the Swahili towns. Often these were Bantu-speaking farming people such as the Pokomo, Giriama, Digo, and Makonde. These diverse peoples traded with the Swahili towns and sometimes worked in them as well.

SOFALA

The winds used for sailing are much less reliable on the Sofala coast than farther north. Far fewer Swahili settlements were established there as a result. However, archaeologists—scholars who sutdy how people lived long ago—have discovered what they believe to be an early Swahili site at Chibuene in southern Mozambique. Later towns include Sofala and Mozambique Island. Other Swahili communities have been found on the four Comoros Islands that span the Mozambique channel, off the northern tip of Madagascar.

EARLY HISTORY

The early history of the Swahili begins in about A.D. 800 and spans five centuries. Many Swahili city-states reached the height of their prosperity by approximately 1300.

SWAHILI ORIGINS

Scholars believe that the earliest Swahili were probably Bantu-speaking farmers who moved from the west to the coast about 1,200 years ago. Living on the coast offered special opportunities for food and trade. They established small fishing villages on the islands of the Lamu Archipelago, on Zanzibar Island, and at Kilwa. Scholars believe they may also have built some small settlements on the mainland of present-day Tanzania. The earliest Swahili on the northern Zanj coast might have been influenced by Cushitic-speaking camel or cattle *pastoralists*, such as today's Somali or Oromo peoples.

The earliest Swahili houses were built of mud packed onto wooden frames and had thatched roofs. The people fished, smelted and worked iron into tools, made beads of shell, worked rock crystal, and probably wove cotton. They kept cattle, goats, and chickens. They had access to camels and hunted animals for food. Early Arab historical sources suggest that they might have exported ivory, rhinoceros horn, and skins, all of which were obtained either by the Swahili or by their inland neighbors. In addition, they might have raised African grains such as millet and sorghum.

TRADE AND EXPANSION

By about A.D. 1000 the Swahili had expanded their trade network, and Arab traders had introduced Islam to the region. The Swahili had founded such towns as Mogadishu, Mombasa, and towns off the

Women in Oman, in South Arabia, spin cotton. Cloth was an important import on the Swahili Coast.

coast of Tanzania on the islands of Pemba and Mafia.

Trade with Arabs and other peoples from the East flourished. The Swahili obtained many products from the African interior to sell, including gold, ivory, rhinoceros horn, rock crystal, animal skins, timber, frankincense, and myrrh. They also traded products from the coast itself: tortoiseshell, ambergris (a waxy substance from whales that is used in perfumes), mangrove poles, cloth, grain and other farm products, salt, and jewelry. Items such as glazed ceramics, silk and cotton cloth, glassware, beads, metal objects, and a great variety of other items were imported into East Africa from overseas.

Swahili towns grew and prospered from this coastal trade. The Swahili became widely known as merchants, and trade became one of the defining characteristics of their society. Gradually, the Swahili established a monopoly on trade along the entire length of the Swahili Coast.

SHIPS

Various kinds of vessels carried trade goods to and from Swahili ports. Sewn boats, which were built without nails, were probably the earliest type of vessel used. The planks of these boats were sewn together with cord made from coconut fibers, and their single rectangular sail was made from woven palm leaves. Sometimes shipbuilders lengthened the bows to resemble a beak or snout and painted "eyes" on them. Although difficult to sail, these sewn boats were surprisingly sturdy. By the twentieth century, sewn vessels were no longer used in East Africa. They had been widely used in the

A man directs the launch of a new boat on the Swahili Coast as others move it over rollers made of mangrove poles.

western Indian Ocean for more than two thousand years.

The word *dhow* applies to a wide variety of Arab-designed ships that were used by the Swahili and their Arab trading partners. The wooden hulls of the dhows were nailed together, and the hulls were fitted with movable, triangular cloth sails called *lateen sails*. These movable sails enabled the boats to cross the ocean without a need for the wind to blow only from behind. This was a technological breakthrough that European shipbuilders achieved only several centuries later. Dhows are still used in the Indian Ocean, but overseas trade is now often carried on motorized ships.

The Swahili also used outriggers. An outrigger is a float or ski that is attached parallel to the boat to provide stability. Outriggers were introduced to East Africa by peoples from Indonesia who settled on the island of Madagascar off the coast of Africa. Outrigger canoes are used on the Swahili coast for fishing or carrying small cargoes between Swahili settlements.

Swahili sailors and those sailing to East Africa used a variety of navigation methods. The Chinese introduced the *magnetic compass* into their travels over the Indian Ocean. Seafarers also navigated by the stars. Those who sailed up and down the coast memorized poems that included sailing directions and descriptions of prominent land features along trading routes. Over the centuries the Swahili gained an international reputation as excellent seafarers.

ISLAM IN EAST AFRICA

Islam—a defining feature of Swahili culture—seems to have been embraced on the islands of the Swahili Coast around 900. When the Arab geographer al-Masudi visited the Swahili Coast in the early 900s, he observed only a few Muslims on the offshore islands. More than two hundred years later, an Arab named al-Idrisi reported that most of the mainland peoples on the East African coast still did not follow Islam.

The earliest physical evidence of Islam found by archaeologists in East Africa is a stone building at Shanga, on an island off the coast of Kenya. It is clearly a mosque. Beneath this stone structure, which dates to about A.D. 1000, are a series of

This elderly man from Zanzibar wears Muslim dress: a white gown, or *kanzu*, and an embroidered hat, called a *kofia*.

older, wooden buildings that may have served as mosques as much as one century earlier.

Islam gradually spread to the mainland, but not everyone in the towns became Muslim. International trade probably promoted the spread of Islam. Muslim merchants visiting East Africa probably preferred to trade with people who shared their religious beliefs.

Swahili towns were generally ruled by a sultan, or Muslim ruler, but a council of elders also held important power in government.

LOCAL HISTORIES

A number of the Swahili coastal towns possess recorded histories. The Kilwa *chronicle*, for example, dates to the early sixteenth century. It exists in both Arabic and Portuguese versions, and each offers a somewhat different view.

In the Arabic version of the Kilwa chronicle, a sultan from Shiraz in the Persian Gulf came with six of his sons to the East African coast. There each of them settled in a major town, including Kilwa, Mafia, Manda, Pemba, and Anjuan in the Comoros.

The port of Moroni on the main island of the Comoros Islands. The white mosque dominates this view of the shore.

When one of the sultan's sons, Ali ibn al-Hasan, reached Kilwa—perhaps in the eleventh or twelfth century—the island was ruled by an African king. At that time it had one resident Muslim family and one mosque.

Ali ibn al-Hasan bought the island for the price of the amount of colored cloth needed to encircle it. He established a dynasty on Kilwa, and then went to the nearby island of Mafia.

In the Portuguese version of the chronicle, Ali ibn al-Hasan was the son of a Persian prince and an African mother. With his wife and family and a few attendants, he sailed first to Mogadishu and Barawa (in Somalia) and then to Kilwa. Once there, the events described in the Portuguese text are similar to those in the Arabic version.

We will probably never know for certain whether the events in either version of the Kilwa chronicle actually occurred or which version is more accurate. Where both versions agree they appear to be more reliable.

The Kilwa chronicle provides an interesting account of how Muslims came to East Africa, found communities already settled there, and established themselves. Muslim immigrants probably intermarried with the local people and became Swahili.

THE SWAHILI COAST IN THE GOLDEN AGE

The Golden Age of the Swahili spanned the fourteenth and fifteenth centuries. Hundreds of Swahili trading towns of all sizes flourished along the coast. The largest of these, such as Pate, Mombasa, Mogadishu, and Kilwa, were city-states.

In 1415, Swahili ambassadors visited the emperor of China, taking gifts of a live giraffe, a zebra, and a "celestial stag" (probably an African antelope) from the Zanj coast. The emperor himself went to the palace gate in Nanjing to meet the giraffe, which was seen as a sign of heaven's favor and proof of the emperor's virtue. A Chinese fleet returned the ambassadors to the Swahili Coast in 1418. The diplomatic visit to China was clearly a success because we know that other Chinese ships later sailed to East Africa on business.

DOING BUSINESS

In Swahili towns, overseas trade was usually based on personal relationships. Instead of conducting business in open public markets, local traders and merchants invited foreign traders into their homes.

Ibn Battuta, a widely traveled Arab who visited the Swahili Coast in 1331, described his experience. When he sailed into Mogadishu, small boats came out to meet the ship. Men came aboard carrying covered dishes of food and invited the merchants to their homes. If the Swahili and Arab traders arranged a satisfactory trading deal, they would continue business with each other year after year. It was customary all along the Swahili Coast for a father to marry off his daughter to an Arab merchant, which would strengthen their trading relationship.

THE SULTAN OF MOGADISHU

Ibn Battuta described Mogadishu as a city with many wealthy merchants. He described the food he

A young Muslim woman from the Swahili Coast

was served there: rice cooked with butter and served with stews made of chicken, meat, fish, and vegetables. He met the sultan, who was carried on a platform supported by four poles. It was covered with a silk canopy and topped with golden birds.

The sultan wore clothes of Egyptian linen and green material from Jerusalem, with a silk sash around his waist and a large turban. Government officials, military commanders, Islamic lawyers, and prominent citizens traveled with him on Fridays, when he held public meetings. A band with drums, trumpets, and flutes often played on these occasions.

A SWAHILI PALACE

Many of the great Swahili cities contained grand works of architecture, such as mosques, monumental tombs, and great palaces.

Nowhere on the coast was there a finer palace than that at Kilwa: the sultan's palace called Husuni Kubwa, meaning great fort. It combined the functions of lavish living quarters with a trading establishment. The sultan controlled all transactions in Kilwa, and the palace was a commercial establishment where merchants came. Covering more than

The sultan's palace at Gedi, in Kenya, is typical of palaces on the Swahili Coast. Above, the court at the center of the palace ruins where trade and politics were probably conducted.

an acre (0.4 hectares) and including more than one hundred rooms, Husuni Kubwa had a great court close to the center that was probably a storage and trading facility. The sultan's living quarters included a unique octagonal bathing pool.

Kilwa attained its greatest prosperity when it controlled the gold trade from mines located to the south. By 1300, gold mined from trading states in the African interior, such as Great Zimbabwe, was sent to Sofala. From Sofala the gold was shipped to Kilwa, where it entered international trade networks. In exchange for gold, traders brought goods from all over the Indian Ocean and the Islamic world, filling the coffers of Husuni Kubwa and the sultan of Kilwa.

A more typical palace is found at Gedi, a site of 47 acres (19 hectares) on the central Kenya coast. Gedi reached its greatest expansion in about 1500. The palace at Gedi was entered through a monumental archway, after which visitors found themselves in an audience court. From this central area, suites of rooms extended in all directions. In addition to serving as homes, the palaces and great homes of Gedi and other Swahili cities were probably also the sites of trade, governmental meetings, law courts, and political discussions.

GREAT MOSQUES

A mosque is the place of worship for Muslims as well as a place for rest, relaxation, social activities, and meetings. The larger Swahili communities had, and still have, a large communal mosque for Friday

The mosque at Gedi, Kenya. In the foreground are the well and facilities for washing oneself before prayer.

prayers, called the Friday mosque, and a number of smaller mosques for daily rituals. Each Swahili town made a special effort to build an impressive Friday mosque because this structure was the focus of community life.

The Friday Mosque at Kilwa has been called the finest medieval mosque in East Africa. The earliest part of the mosque dates from the twelfth century. Later, a large southern addition was erected with a beautiful roof containing thirty domes. Like most

The unique features of the coral tombs of the Swahili Coast—such as their towering columns—still puzzle experts. The tall column is 24 feet (8 m) high and once held a fifteenth-century Chinese bowl as a decoration.

East African mosques, it includes water tanks fed by nearby wells for washing oneself before entering and an arched recess in the north wall to point out the direction of Mecca, the holy city.

GREAT PILLARS

Monumental tombs are a unique feature of East African architecture. These tombs were rectangular buildings of coral *masonry*. Large columns, decorated with beautiful ceramics from the Islamic world and the Far East, were often built above the eastern wall. Sometimes large tombstones or other monuments were set upon the walls instead of columns.

The largest tomb on the coast, in northern Kenya, is the size of a small house. The tallest column stood 33 feet (10 m) high on a tomb at Bur Gao, Somalia.

The motivation for building the great columns is not known. No large tomb has been fully excavated, so it is also unknown how many persons may have been buried in such tombs. Today, people treat many of the tombs as sacred places and go there to pray, burn incense, and leave offerings.

Other ancient tombs found on the Swahili Coast are domed. They often have small doors on one side, giving them the appearance of little houses.

EVERYDAY LIFE IN THE GOLDEN AGE

By 1500 Swahili civilization flourished from Mogadishu to Kilwa and even farther south. As trade thrived, Swahili communities blossomed. Each city had its own distinct character—a unique blend of local peoples, products, architecture, and environments.

SWAHILI CITIES

In a typical Swahili community, the houses of the wealthier members of the community were built from coral masonry. These houses surrounded the Friday mosque at the center of town. Beyond the masonry houses were the homes of the less

A view of the ruins of Pate, showing the massive walls typical of Swahili towns

wealthy. These structures were made of mud and timber and had thatched roofs. They were comfortable, although simpler and less sturdy than the stone houses.

Towns and cities were often located along a beach or harbor. They were usually surrounded by a wall of stone masonry standing 6 or 7 feet high (2 m). Entrance to the town was through gates in the wall.

DAILY LIFE

Life along the Swahili Coast followed the rhythm of the Muslim day, which requires prayer five times daily. Before dawn, a *muezzin* at the mosque would wake the community with a call to prayer. Men went to the mosque, washed their hands and faces and rinsed their mouths, removed their shoes, and entered to pray.

After a breakfast of rice, cakes, or eggs, the daily work began. The Swahili ideal has long been that of a trader, so many persons would buy and sell merchandise in their homes or open their shops for business. The less affluent men followed a variety of trades, such as boat builders, fishermen, mangrove cutters, tailors, masons, carpenters, farmers, or blacksmiths. The more influential men in the community were Muslim traders, government officials, judges, lawyers, and teachers.

In addition to the craftsmen and merchants working in the towns, persons from surrounding villages came to town to trade. They supplied food to town merchants and provided for the foreign trade such items as ivory, skins, rhinoceros horn, timber, and grains. In return, they received manufactured goods or other items of equal value.

Morning business hours ended at noon for midday prayer, lunch, and an afternoon rest during

Swahili settlements on the coast traded and had cultural interaction with inland peoples, such as the ancestors of this man wearing a ceremonial mask.

the heat of the day. Business resumed in the late afternoon. It halted for prayer at sunset, and then continued during the early evening.

Women tended the home and dealt with domestic duties: overseeing the household, rearing children, and preparing food. In more conservative communities women were expected to wear veils when they left the house. Women gathered in homes during the afternoon to talk about the day's happenings or in the evening while the men chatted at the mosques.

A wealthier man wore imported colored cottons and silks or a pure white gown, a turban, and leather sandals. A silver dagger hung from a sash at his waist. In addition to imported fabrics, the coast had its own local cotton-weaving industry. Many women wore colored clothes, but devout Muslim women generally wore dark-colored garments with veils.

SWAHILI HOUSES

Swahili masonry houses in the Golden Age were comfortable and sometimes elaborate buildings. Houses consisted of several long rooms arranged one behind the other. Visitors were entertained only in the front area of the house. Privacy increased as one passed from the front to the rear of the house. Back rooms were for family only. Children's beds were placed at the ends of the long rooms. The rear room of the house was for the head of the household and his wife.

The simplest stone houses were about three rooms deep and usually had an interior toilet and a storage room. More complex houses had courtyards, passageways, and rooms divided into smaller chambers. Most houses were a single story, but some during the Golden Age were two stories high.

The inner chambers of the wealthy homes were decorated with panels of decorative plaster *niches* on the back and end walls of rooms. Precious crockery, the family Koran (the holy book of Islam), and other valuables were kept in these niches. Rooms were lit by burning oil in ceramic lamps.

Cooking was done in the front rooms of houses, in open courtyards, or in special kitchen sheds outside the house. Ceramic ovens were set into the ground for baking cakes of sorghum or millet.

The narrow streets of Lamu are typical of Swahili towns.

Other cooking was done in bowls, on earthenware stoves, or over open fires. A Swahili dinner might include rice cooked in coconut milk served with fish, chicken or goat meat, drinks made from citrus fruits or *tamarind*, and bananas and mangoes for dessert.

Besides daily activities, at least two important rituals took place in the house. During the marriage ceremony, the bride was prepared for the event in the home. There, the most important part of the ceremony took place when the bride, wearing beautiful makeup, clothes, and precious silver jewelry, was seated below the array of niches in the private back room and presented to the female wedding guests. The other ritual use for the rear room of the house was to prepare the bodies of the dead for burial. The deceased was washed, wrapped in clean linen, and then taken to the cemetery for burial.

5 FOREIGN POWERS

The Portuguese entered the western Indian Ocean in 1498. They hoped to open a sea route for importing spices from Asia to Europe, because the overland route had been blocked by the Arabs and Turks. Once in East Africa, the Portuguese soon recognized many trading opportunities there, including gold. They built alliances with some sultans and demanded tribute from the major Swahili cities. The Portuguese desire for riches of any kind disrupted the traditional Swahili trade routes and caused rivalries among the Swahili communities. This led to warfare.

The Portuguese established their main center

Many Arab traders, such as these merchants in Saudi Arabia, still specialize in gold. Much of their gold supply still comes from Africa, but no longer from the Swahili Coast.

of operations at Goa on the west coast of India in the sixteenth century. To control East Africa, they built forts, garrisons, customhouses, and churches in the Swahili cities, including Kilwa, Malindi, Mombasa, and Pate. They set up their southern headquarters at Mozambique Island, where the construction of the fortress of San Sebastiaõ started in 1558.

The Portuguese military occupation of the Swahili Coast was often brutal. Within twenty years of their arrival at the coast, the Portuguese had sacked Kilwa and destroyed not only its role in the gold trade but also its economic power. They forced the large towns to pay an annual tribute in the form of money and goods, and they imposed customs duties on imports and exports passing through Swahili towns. Some Swahili towns yielded to Portuguese rule; those that rebelled were treated harshly. The Portuguese looted and burned many towns and often executed Swahili leaders.

In 1585 and again in 1588, Turkish raiders visited the East African coast. They were enemies of the Portuguese and urged the northern Swahili towns to revolt against the Portuguese. These uprisings were crushed by the Portuguese.

Having imposed their power on the southern section of the Swahili Coast, the Portuguese set their sights on controlling the northern part of the coast. With this in mind, they began building a massive fort in Mombasa, one of the wealthiest and

Fort Jesus, Mombasa, in Kenya

most important cities on the coast at that time. Named Fort Jesus, it was one of the largest Portuguese forts in Africa and held many soldiers. One of their chief goals was to seize Pate, the leading city on the northern coast, which covered more than 70 acres (28 hectares). Within its massive town walls were numerous mosques and impressive houses and tombs.

The leaders of Pate tried unsuccessfully to reach an agreement with the Portuguese. After this, Pate became a leader in trying to oust the Portuguese invaders from the coast. The Portuguese punished Pate with five brutal attacks between 1637 and 1687.

The Swahili towns never presented a united front to the Portuguese. During the seventeenth century, however, the powerful Arabian sultanate of Oman became allied with their Swahili trading partners. The Omani crushed Portuguese power in East Africa. In 1698, after a three-year siege, Fort Jesus fell to the Omani and their Swahili allies. The Portuguese briefly reoccupied Fort Jesus in 1728 and 1729, but their hold over East Africa had been broken by the end of the seventeenth century.

The two-hundred-year Portuguese occupation had devastated the Swahili Coast. The delicate web of Swahili trading networks, developed over centuries, had been damaged beyond repair. Kilwa was ruined. Pate and Mombasa, having endured the brunt of the conflict with the Portuguese, were devastated. Almost none of the larger Swahili settlements remained unscathed. Many towns survived, but many others that had been inhabited for centuries were abandoned forever.

It is possible that drought and warfare with mainland African groups may also have contributed to the downfall of some of these Swahili settlements. Undoubtedly, however, the disruption of trade by the Portuguese and the unstable political climate they created were major causes of the decline of the Swahili Coast.

OMANI INFLUENCE

In 1727 Mombasa came under the rule of the Mazrui family from Oman. By the 1750s, the Mazrui had become independent of Omani rule and led Mombasa to a new prosperity. Some Swahili cities chafed under Mazrui control and instead remained loyal to the rulers of Oman itself.

Late in the century Zanzibar came under direct Omani rule. Led by the al-Busaid family, which had its headquarters in Zanzibar, the Omani gradually extended their influence up and down the coast. In the early 1800s, Pate and Lamu came under their influence. Mazrui power in

A carved door in Oman is similar to those found in Zanzibar. This illustrates the close ties between Oman and the Swahili Coast.

Mombasa shrank correspondingly. By 1840 Busaidi dominance over the coast was supreme under the leadership of Sayyid Said, who moved his seat of government to Zanzibar at this time.

SLAVERY

Records of a rebellion of enslaved Africans in the Persian Gulf region in A.D. 696 prove that Africans from East Africa or perhaps the Sudan had been imported there at that early date. The sale of enslaved Africans from East Africa to the Islamic world, India, and as far away as China continued until the 1800s, when it reached its height. The trade was first run by inland Bantu groups (such as the Nyamwezi, Yao, and Kamba). By the 1850s, however, Swahili caravans from Zanzibar were traveling as far as the great lakes of central Africa and the Congo to buy ivory and slaves.

In 1873 the Sultan of Zanzibar, under pressure from the British, outlawed the export of slaves. Slavery itself was abolished in 1897 in Zanzibar and Tanganyika (which together today make up Tanzania). It was outlawed in neighboring Kenya in 1907.

African slaves on the Swahili Coast await transport.

EUROPEAN COLONIZATION

By the end of the 1800s, European power in Africa was on the rise. In 1890 Zanzibar became a British protectorate. Eventually, southern Somalia became an Italian colony, Kenya became a British colony, and Tanganyika—at first a German colony—became a British colony after World War I. Mozambique was a Portuguese possession.

After much struggle against European colonial powers, these countries and the Swahili peoples within them regained their independence in the 1960s and 1970s.

6 THE SWAHILI TODAY

Today, the Swahili peoples continue to adapt to new influences even as they retain a strong sense of the cultural traditions developed over twelve centuries.

Such cities as Lamu, Malindi, and Mombasa in Kenya, and Zanzibar and Dar es Salaam in Tanzania continue to bustle with Swahili trade. Swahili influence is still felt strongly in the Comoros Islands and less strongly in Somalia and Mozambique. Many Swahili still follow the traditional occupation of trading as merchants, storekeepers, and international import/export traders.

Today the Swahili create distinctive arts and crafts. These include beautiful wood carving, silver

A man blows a 17th-century *silwa*, a trumpet used on special occasions such as weddings and state ceremonies. Made of ivory, it has a carved inscription from the Koran—revealing its links with both Africa and the Islamic world. It is kept in the Lamu Museum.

jewelry, decorative plasterwork on buildings, and illustrated Korans. Building boats—from small fishing vessels to large, ocean-going vessels of many tons—remains an important occupation among the Swahili.

Traditional dress is still worn in most places on

the Swahili Coast. Men generally wear white gowns and beautifully embroidered hats, while women dress in black robes and wear veils in public. Boys continue to attend mosque schools for instruction in the teachings of Islam and also receive a Western-style education.

The Swahili language has become one of the major African languages. It is spoken both on the East African coast and in the interior, where people from different ethnic groups often use Swahili as a shared second language. Some Swahili words have even become part of the English language: *safari,* a trip or expedition; *simba,* a lion; and *kwanzaa,* which means first or beginning, and which has become the name of an annual African American cultural and educational event held at the New Year.

As always, Swahili communities include many non-Swahili neighbors. In Lamu today one might encounter Pokomo farmers from the Tana River area, Giriama from the Malindi area, Boni hunters and gatherers, European tourists, Bantu-speaking peoples from the Nairobi area, and perhaps visitors from southern Arabia or the Persian Gulf.

A Muslim boy from the Swahili Coast

Swahili cities, it seems, have always been characterized by this mix of Swahili peoples, neighboring peoples, and foreigners. It continues to make the cities of the Swahili vibrant places.

TIMELINE

A.D. 750-850	Earliest Swahili cities founded at Kilwa, Manda, Pate, and Shanga
900s	Arab geographer al-Masudi describes the peoples and products of the East African coast and notes the presence of few Muslims on the islands
1000	Earliest mosque built on the coast, at Shanga; Mombasa founded
1100s	First building of the Great Mosque at Kilwa
1300s	Husuni Kubwa built at Kilwa
1331	Arab traveler Ibn Battuta visits and describes Mogadishu, Mombasa, and Kilwa
1417-1422	Large Chinese fleets visit East Africa twice
1498	Portuguese arrive in East Africa
1505	Portuguese sack Kilwa
1585, 1588	Turkish raiders incite Swahili cities to resist Portuguese
1593-1596	Portuguese build Fort Jesus in Mombasa
1600s	Height of Swahili resistance to Portuguese at Pate
1698	Fort Jesus falls to Omani and their Swahili allies
1700s	Mazrui family from Oman rule Mombasa
1800s	Rise of al-Busaid power in Zanzibar and along the coast
1873-1907	Slavery outlawed in East Africa
1960s-1970s	Kenya, Mozambique, Somalia, and Tanzania win independence
Present	Swahili culture flourishes, Swahili language is widely used

GLOSSARY

Bantu group of languages spoken in central, southern, and much of eastern Africa

chronicle continuous narrative, usually a historical account

city-state self-ruled city that also rules surrounding territory

Cushitic group of languages spoken by nomadic peoples in the northern parts of eastern Africa

dhow Arab boat with triangular cloth, or lateen, sails

Islam religion that holds that Allah is the one God

lateen sail movable triangular sail

magnetic compass device with a magnetic needle pointing to the pole; used in navigation

mangrove bush-like tree of the East African sea coasts

masonry stonework or brickwork

mosque Islamic house of worship

muezzin Muslim crier who calls the hour of daily prayers

multifaceted having many aspects

niche alcove in a wall

pastoralist person who herds livestock to earn a living

Roman alphabet set of letters originated by the ancient Romans; now used by most Western languages

tamarind kind of fruit

worldview comprehensive way of looking at the world from a specific point of view

FOR FURTHER READING

Department of Geography, Lerner Publications. *Tanzania in Pictures.* Minneapolis, MN: Lerner Group, 1989.

Farmer, Nancy. *Do You Know Me?* New York: Orchard Books Watts, 1993.

Hussein, Ikram. *Teenage Refugees from Somalia Speak Out.* New York: Rosen Publishing Group, 1997.

FOR ADVANCED READERS

Brown, Dale, ed. *Africa's Glorious Legacy.* Alexandria, VA: Time-Life Books, 1994.

Maren, Michael. *The Land and People of Kenya.* New York: HarperCollins Children's Books, 1989.

Middleton, John. *The World of the Swahili: An African Mercantile Civilization.* New Haven: Yale University Press, 1994.

WEB SITES

Due to the changeable nature of the Internet, sites appear and disappear very quickly. Internet addresses must be entered with capital and lowercase letters exactly as they appear.

University of Pennsylvania—African Studies WWW:
http://www.sas.upenn.edu/African_Studies/AS.html

Kenya Web: http://www.kenyaweb.com/

Kiswahili Home Page: http://conn.me.queensu.ca/kassim/documents/kiswa/swahili.htm

INDEX

ABOUT THE AUTHOR

Thomas H. Wilson is director of the Logan Museum of Anthropology and the Wright Museum of Art at Beloit College in Beloit, Wisconsin. He earned a Ph.D. in anthropology at the University of California–Berkeley and for five years served as coastal archaeologist for the National Museums of Kenya. Wilson lived on the island of Lamu, conducted archaeological research along the entire length of the Kenyan coast, and excavated at Pate, Takwa, and other Swahili sites. He has written and spoken extensively about Swahili archaeology, history, culture, and architecture.